7 Financial Truths You Need to Know

And How They Make the Difference Between
Prosperity and Government Dependency

Michael P. Cutbirth

Michael P. Cutbirth
Richmond, TX

Michael P. Cutbirth
Richmond, TX

www.Michael-Cutbirth.com

Ordering Information:
Quantity sales. Special discounts may be available on quantity purchases by corporations, associations, and others. For details, michael@michael-cutbirth.com.

7 Financial Truths You Need to Know
Michael P. Cutbirth —1st ed.
ISBN 978-0-578-68591-5

Disclaimer

This book is a teaching tool and is for educational purposes only. Past performance and numbers cited do not guarantee future results, and the views expressed in it are mine alone. While I freely share my knowledge throughout this book, and share what has worked for me, I can't guarantee you (or anyone) specific results from reading this (or any) book. Because of that, neither myself nor the publisher accepts any liability in any form as a result of reading this book.

Now, with that being shared, know this: I have faith in you, and all investors that, with the right information, help, and action you can accomplish your financial goals and dreams. Enjoy the book, dear reader!

Disclosure

Michael Cutbirth is a registered representative of Lincoln Financial Securities Corp. Securities offered through Lincoln Financial Securities Corp., a broker/dealer (member SIPC). Investment advisory services offered through Lincoln Financial Securities a registered investment advisor.

Marketing names used in the book are associated with the individual authors and are not an affiliate of Lincoln Financial Securities.

Lincoln Financial Securities Corp. and its representatives do not provide legal or tax advice. You may want to consult a legal or tax advisor regarding any legal or tax information as it relates to your personal circumstances.

The material here reflects the views of the author and not necessarily those of Lincoln Financial Securities or its affiliates. This material is intended for educational purposes only and should not be used as investment advice or recommendations.

This book highlights important industry regulations and concepts. Please review these resources and concepts and consult your tax, financial and legal professionals before implementing or making changes in a retirement plan.

Table of Contents

To my wife, Dana, who is always by my side, and to our amazing children, Joshua, Sara, Jeni, and Hannah, and our grandchildren, Robert, June, and Henry. You all inspire me and motivate me every day.

To my good buddy, Don Blanton; words cannot describe what learning from you the past 23 years has meant to my career, to me and to my family. You are the one who taught me the truth about money and how it really works.

INTRODUCTION

If what you thought to be true about the government, taxes, and the financial services industry turned out not to be true, when would you want to know?

In the Gospel of John, we're told, "You shall know the truth, and the truth shall set you free," (John 8:32). What a beautiful, prosperous, loving world we could all enjoy and flourish in if everyone simply told the truth. Not half-truths or partial truths, but the entire truth.

I'm from a small town, a bit northeast of Houston, called Crosby, Texas. Throughout my childhood, I was related to about 80% of that town. With that many eyes on you able to keep track of your every move, you quickly learn to tell the truth.

In fact, my dad, who only had a high school education, gave me one of the best pieces of advice I've ever received. He told me, "Michael, if you never tell a lie, you never have to worry about what you told somebody." That advice has proven to be more priceless than any MasterCard I could have ever owned.

I can't help but think about former President Bill Clinton. He told so many lies and "half-truths" on the campaign trail that there was no way he could ever remember what he actually said the week before (or sometimes the day before) each campaign stop.

Here's another "whopper" for you: "With our plan, if you like your doctor, you can keep your doctor, **and** your medical premiums and costs will go down." Really? How'd that work out for us, America? And now, that former community organizer, who always said he was just an "average American" lives in a $14.85 million mansion. If that's the case, sign me up!

How much faster, easier, and more confidently could we invest our hard-earned money if we could simply trust the advice of financial advisors we work with and everything we hear on the business cable television shows to be the absolute truth? Wow. Think of how stress-free the world of politics and business would be if everyone just told the truth, or, at the very least when giving their opinions or "best guesses," just say so. Why don't more journalists name their source(s)? What a game-changer that would be.

This year, my college sweetheart and I will be celebrating our 40th wedding anniversary as well as our 40-year college class reunion. Through the grace of God, we raised and put four children through private elementary school, public high school, and all four are college graduates. We did this all on one income.

I've made pretty much every financial mistake one can make including running up credit card debt into the tens of thousands of dollars without being able to pay it off, thus wasting **thousands** in interest expense. Believe me, we've had much less financial stress the past 20 to 25 years since we began paying our credit card bills in full each month.

Here are a few of my personal beliefs I've gleaned over almost 35 years of helping people with their finances:

I believe that every person in this country only needs to pay income tax on their money ONE time, just once - that's as you earn it. Where you choose to invest your money after you've already paid income tax determines how many **more** times you allow your money to be taxed. Think dividends, interest, capital gains, and 1099 income. "Michael, can you help me find better strategies to build my wealth?" Absolutely. Keep reading.

I also believe people ought to be in control of their hard-earned money and not just blindly follow what the federal government, Wall Street, or financial institutions recommend we do with our money. Let's be honest here. Do you **really** believe they have your best interests at heart? Do you really think they design the rules so you and I win? I don't think so.

I believe income tax rates will increase in the future and the government, like Robin Hood, will take it from the rich. It's the government who defines who is rich, and is the government your friend? Probably not.

Do you think the best way to save for your retirement is to max out your annual contribution to your 401(k) plan? If your first instinct is, "Yes," I have a question for you: What tax bracket are you going to be in throughout the 10, 20, or 30 years of your retirement?

I believe the world economy changed in 2008, but Wall Street, and the mutual fund industry, didn't advise the average investor to change anything about how they invest. The mantra remained "max out your 401(k) and don't worry, the market always comes back." Sounds good, but is it the truth?

You may be wondering why I wrote this book. It all goes back to John 8:32, "You shall know the truth, and the truth shall set you free." Being analytical, my favorite question is "Why?"

If the financial crisis of 2008 was caused by some type of illegal financial manipulation, why wasn't anyone put in jail? Why does the mutual fund industry continue to recommend a "buy and hold" investment strategy for individual investors when, on average, every seven years since the 1960s the stock market has dropped 20% or more? Over my 30 plus years of experience in the financial services business, I just wanted to know how wealth really works.

I've listened to many money managers and economists, read hundreds of financial magazines and books, and listened to countless keynote speakers and colleagues tell me what they think is the best way to help my clients be financially successful. I discovered recently that most of these people were all pitifully wrong. They all had good intentions, but they were all teaching me to build paper wealth for my clients using math.

I wrote this book for the average investor because I firmly believe that if they don't make a few fundamental changes in the way they invest, they're headed for financial failure. The federal government is not your friend. Wall Street is not your friend. In the balance of this book, I will make my case as to what things have changed and give you a few ideas how you might adjust your thinking and investment strategy so that you are in control. Are you a person who likes to be in control when it comes to your money, or be at the mercy of the federal government? If you're one who wants to be in control, keep reading.

Open your mind. Buckle your seat belt. Let's begin to examine and repair the future potholes in your road to overall financial success.

CHAPTER 1

What the Government Doesn't Want You to Know and Why It's NOT Your Friend

The federal government is not your friend. I repeat, *the federal government is not your friend.* This country is so evenly split politically that it boggles the mind.

Were you aghast, like many Americans, when some liberal-minded members of Congress like Maxine Waters recommended people confront conservative politicians and their supporters during the presidential election of 2016? What does it say about our country when a 60-year-old man wearing a red cap that stated, "Happy Birthday, I'm 60," gets physically struck in the face from behind because it resembled a "Make America Great Again" cap? It's incredibly sad.

Consider this: normally, a sitting president is reelected and serves eight years. Then the opposing party candidate usually wins the election following and serves the next eight years. During your retirement, the federal government determines and sets the amount of income taxes you'll pay on every single dollar you withdraw from your IRA every single year. Given the probability you're not going to like the president about half the time, is this being in control of your money or out of control?

America, the federal government produces nothing. The federal government operates zero corporations or small businesses. The federal government produces zero products sold in the marketplace. The federal government's only source of revenue is income taxes. As Yoda from Star Wars would put it, "Remember young Skywalker, the government it is that defines who's rich."

The "government it is" that not only controls the tax rates but changes them whenever they need more tax revenue at their sole discretion without ever asking our opinions before doing so. Don't believe me?

Year	Initial Rate	Threshold for Lowest Bracket	Top Rate	Threshold for Highest Bracket
1940	4.00%	$4,000	81.10%	$5,000,000
1941	10.00%	$2,000	81.00%	$5,000,000
1942	19.00%	$2,000	88.00%	$200,000
1943	19.00%	$2,000	88.00%	$200,000
1944	23.00%	$2,000	94.00%	$200,000
1945	23.00%	$2,000	94.00%	$200,000
1946	19.00%	$2,000	86.45%	$200,000
1947	19.00%	$2,000	86.45%	$200,000
1948	16.60%	$4,000	82.13%	$400,000
1949	16.60%	$4,000	82.12%	$400,000
1950	17.40%	$4,000	84.36%	$400,000
1951	20.40%	$4,000	91.00%	$400,000
1952	22.20%	$4,000	92.00%	$400,000
1953	22.20%	$4,000	92.00%	$400,000
1954	29.00%	$4,000	91.00%	$400,000

Going back to 1941, to be in the top tax bracket of 81%, you had to be making $5 million a year. That's a lot of cheese even today, but back then, a very small percentage of Americans had incomes of $5 million or more. In 1942, after Japan bombed Pearl Harbor and America was forced into World War II, the top tax rate increased from 81% to 88%. In addition, the government also decreased the amount of income needed to be in the top tax bracket from $5 million to $200,000. (How's that for changing the definition of "rich?") That's a decrease of $4.8 million and led to a much greater number of Americans who paid more in income taxes. Inconceivable!

If you don't think the government would ever do that, again, remember these wise words, "Fool me once, shame on you. Fool me twice, shame on me." One other fact: that $200,000 "government definition" of who's rich remained constant from 1941 to 1947 when the government "graciously" doubled the definition of who's rich to $400,000, where it stayed for 14 years (before being reduced back to $200,000 in 1965).

You may be thinking, "It's okay for the rich to pay more income taxes. They have money, but I'll never be rich." Well, let's examine how graciously the government treated the poor.

In 1940 the lowest tax rate was 4.4% for anyone with $4,000 of taxable income. In 1941, the income threshold was cut in half to $2,000 of income **and** the lowest tax rate more than doubled from 4.4% to 10%. The federal government taxing authority is an equal opportunity offender. Both rich and poor pay more.

To add insult to injury in 1942, when World War II ramped up, the government's income definition of who's “poor” stayed at $2,000 but they almost doubled the minimum tax rate again from 10% to 19%. The government bumped it again to 23% for 1944 and 1945. This whole time, $2,000 remained the government's income definition of who's poor.

“You shall know the truth, and the truth shall set you free.”

Most Americans begin to contribute to an IRA or 401(k) soon after they join the workforce. Here is an example to illustrate: let's assume the average age for an American to start saving money for retirement is 30. Let's further assume their tax filing status is “married filing jointly,” and most have purchased, or will soon purchase, their first home and have one or two children, or will soon begin a family.

Will this be a period when they're in a high or low tax bracket? Probably a lower tax bracket, right? If that’s the case, how in the world can their IRA and 401(k) contributions put in at their lowest tax bracket ever be withdrawn, 35 to 40 years later, at a similarly low tax bracket?

Want more pain? Upon the death of the first spouse, all further IRA withdrawals are taxed at "single" tax rates. And are those lower or higher than at "married filing jointly" rates? In reality, those rates are almost double. And the IRA RMD, or Required Minimum Distribution (the amount the government requires you to take out each year), for the surviving spouse's IRA graciously decreases, right? Wrong, it stays the same. From that point on, the contributions made at lower "married filing jointly" tax rates are withdrawn at the maximum "single filing" tax rate unless one remarries or has little to no balance of funds in their IRA.

I believe that income tax rates (and, in turn, income taxes) will have to go up in the future for two main reasons.

First, the government's debt is currently about $24 trillion and increasing according to the US Treasury as of early April 2020 (www.usdebtclock.org). This debt is calculated to be about $73,000 per US citizen and almost $194,000 per US taxpayer, according to the same website. In addition, current estimates are that Social Security benefits will start to exceed the program's cost in 2020, and the program's $2.9 trillion reserve fund is estimated to be **depleted** by 2035.

As I see it, there are only four possible solutions, and one of them has the proverbial "snowball's chance in hell" of being implemented: the federal government stops spending more money than they are taking in. The second possible solution is to increase the amount of income that everyone pays Social Security tax on, which is currently limited to $137,700 for tax year 2020. The third possibility is to further delay Social Security retirement age for all generations (hopefully excluding the Baby Boomers because I am one). The fourth possible solution is to increase tax rates for everyone. Do you see yourself winning with any one of these last three? Is there any other solution?

The second main reason I believe income tax rates will go up is a population difference between generations. Consider the chart below with estimated population figures from the year 2017 for each of the generations illustrated.

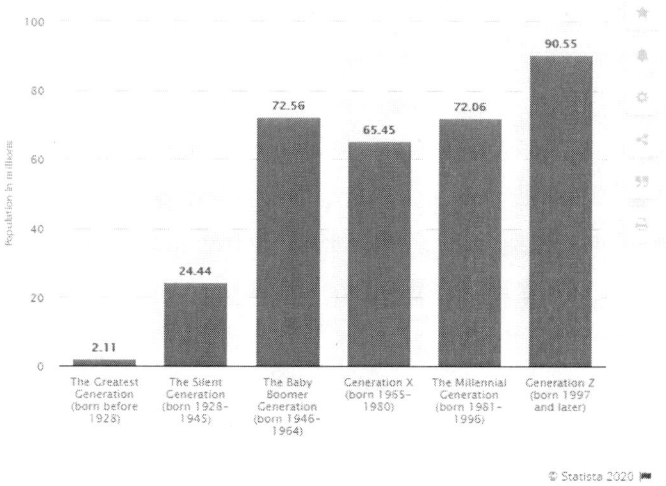

(https://www.statista.com/statistics/797321/us-population-by-generation/)

The reason income tax rates have been able to be kept low, and why Social Security and Medicare funding has been adequate up until recent years, is because 70 to 80 million Baby Boomers were likely employed since about the year 2000. These were the people responsible for paying taxes to support the 20 to 25 million members of the Depression era, or as they're often referred to, the Silent Generation.

America, you better hope and pray that a majority of Baby Boomers work and continue to pay income taxes beyond the normal retirement age of 65 because of these numbers. As you can see, the population of Generation X that follows the Baby Boomers is estimated to be about 65.45 million, or a little more than 7 million **below** the 72.56 million count of the Baby Boomer generation.

Now, if you think the government isn't your friend, Wall Street and the financial services firms certainly are not either. In chapter two, I'll give some examples of how you can further stay in control of your money.

CHAPTER 2

What Financial Services Firms Don't Want You to Know and Why Wall Street is Definitely Not Your Friend Either

Have you ever wondered why the financial services industry always advises investors to stay "fully invested?" Have you also wondered if mutual fund managers follow that same advice?

The primary answer to the first question above is simply management fees. Think about it this way: how much money do the mutual fund companies make from cash and money market funds? Close to zero. And how much do these same companies make through regular mutual funds? A lot more than zero.

Mutual fund companies, through their wholesalers, have done an excellent job of training financial advisors to be their puppets. They teach us to spread their half-truths, or "half the story mantras," to the public. One way these companies do this is by constantly producing charts that show how much lower the average investor's return would have been if they missed the best 10 days during a particular time period.

The funny thing is, in my 35-year career, I've **never** seen a mutual fund company publish a corresponding chart of comparative numbers if you missed the **worst** 10 days during that same time period.

The following tables and commentary illustrate this point.

	Missed Best Days	Missed Worst Days
10 days	4.10 percent	11.23 percent
20 days	2.15 percent	13.80 percent
40 days	-0.93 percent	17.59 percent

Source: "Diversification by Strategy Reduces Risk, Study Show," Hepburn Capital Management. *Past performance does not guarantee future results.*

The first table (previous page) measures the S&P 500 Index from 1983 to 2008. Over that 25-year time period, the average annual return was 7.06%. If you missed the **best** 10 days, your return decreased from 7.06% to 4.10%. If you went on to miss the **best** 20 days, your return decreased to 2.15%. And if you missed the **best** 40 days, your return decreased to a negative 0.93%. Mutual fund companies use this data to support their advice to stay fully invested, but did the average investors make more money following this advice? Let's look at the flipside.

If you were to have missed the **worst** 10 days, your return increased from 7.06% to 11.23%. If you missed the **worst** 20 days, your return increased to 13.8%, almost doubling your return. Finally, if you missed the **worst** 40 days, your return increased to 17.59%! What's the point? Missing the worst days was much more valuable than the cost of missing the best days.

More recent data illustrates the same story. This table (next page) shows the return of the S&P 500 index fund from Index Fund Advisors for the period of 2000 to 2019.

$10,000 Invested in S&P 500 Index Fund	Annualized Return	Value of $10k at End	Gain/ Loss	Impact of Missing Days
All 5,035 Trading Days	6.02%	$32,192.93	$22,192.93	-
Less the 5 biggest gain days	3.87%	$21,359.95	$11,359.95	-48.81%
Less the 10 biggest gain days	2.42%	$16,122.15	$6,122.15	-72.41%
Less the 20 biggest gain days	0.07%	$10,145.77	$145.77	-99.34%
Less the 40 biggest gain days	-3.79%	$4,615.42	-$5,384.58	-124.26%

Source: Index Fund Advisors; Data 01/01/2000 through 12/31/2019

The average return over the past 20 years was 6.02%. If you missed the **best** 10 days, your return decreased from 6.02% to 2.42%. Like before, if you missed the **best** 20 days, your return decreased to 0.07%. And if you missed the **best** 40 days, your return decreased to a negative 3.79%.

$10,000 Invested in S&P 500 Index Fund	Annualized Return	Value of $10k at End	Gain/Loss	Impact of Missing Days
All 5,035 Trading Days	6.02%	$32,192.93	$22,192.93	-
Less the 5 biggest loss days	8.30%	$49.300.06	$39,300.06	77.08%
Less the 10 biggest loss days	10.01%	$67,338.55	$57,338.55	158.36%
Less the 20 biggest loss days	12.81%	$111,428.95	$101,428.95	357.03%
Less the 40 biggest loss days	17.51%	$252,117.29	$242,117.29	990.97%

Source: Index Fund Advisors; Data 01/01/2000 through 12/31/2019

Again, let's look at the flip side. If you missed the **worst** 10 days, your return increased from 6.02% to 10.01%. If you went further and avoided the **worst** 20 days, your return increased to 12.81%, a solid doubling. And, finally, if you missed the **worst** 40 days, your return increased to 17.51% - almost 3 times the "buy and hold" return of 6.02%.

Once again, the table shows that missing the worst days was much more valuable than missing the best days, hands down.

To answer the second question we started with, whether or not mutual fund managers stay invested as they recommend the average investor do, consider the following: according to Morningstar (as of 2016) the average mutual fund had an annual turnover ratio of 89%. That means the average fund manager sells and revises its entire basket of holdings every single year.

Does that sound like buy and hold? Or does it sound more like the advice your parents gave you when you caught them doing something they told you not to do, "Do as I say, not as I do?" Either way, it's another "gotcha."

Do you ever wonder why some mutual fund companies always recommend having a certain percentage of your portfolio invested in international funds and alternative funds (securities other than stocks, bonds, and cash)? Could it possibly be the higher average management fees they collect?

Consider the following table. According to Morningstar, as of 12/31/2018, the asset-weighted average fund fees as a percentage of US equity funds was 0.70% a year. For international equity funds, it was 0.82% a year, for alternative funds, it was 1.31% a year, and for taxable bonds, it was only 0.53% a year.

Asset Class	**Weighted-Average Fee**
US Equities	0.70%
International Equities	0.82%
Alternatives	1.31%
Taxable Bonds	0.53%

Let me share a story with you of how I learned the hard way that mutual fund wholesalers are at times just salespeople, and sometimes their objectives differ greatly from mine and that of my clients, **especially** during a period of a sharp market decline.

It was early 2000 and the "tech bubble" was about halfway through its downward spiral. A wholesaler from a very popular mutual fund company visited me in my office with advice that went something like this: "Our top management team recommends that you keep your clients invested, especially in our "Fab Five" funds, as we're confident they will recover quickly. Remind your clients that the market has always come back from sharp sell-offs, and we're confident history will repeat itself."

Most likely, I was then handed one of their half-truth flyers showing what happens to individual investor returns if they missed the 10 or 20 best days in the market, just as we previously discussed. What this taught me about the importance of mutual funds' management fees in 2001 was repeated during the financial crisis of 2008.

I learned that fund companies make money through management fees. If too many clients want to sell, the fund companies start losing money. The upper management of these companies has a totally different objective in that they want to minimize redemptions. Why? Since their management fees are a major source of revenue for fund companies, they favor stability and ensuring their fees do not drop as sharply as the market. So, invariably, they produce sales material and instructions to their wholesalers that encourage financial advisors to advise their clients to keep their money invested.

The result? This caused me to create another financial belief. I believe we can help our clients more by helping them avoid or minimize their losses than we ever could by helping them try to pick the winners. Because of this, I also developed my "sell philosophy," which I'll share with you in chapter five.

CHAPTER 3

Action Steps to Take Now

We begin this chapter with a focus on the 401(k) plan. Does the name Ted Benna have any meaning to you? If not, it should, because he is the one who invented the 401(k) plan in 1980 while he was an employee with The Johnson Companies in Philadelphia. Funny enough, he later lamented that fact in 2011 when he said that he created a "monster" that should be "blown up."

He went on to say that the plans had grown so over-complicated and so fraught with hidden fees and opportunities for bad decisions that they were better at enriching the financial industry than actual savers!

In fact, the original purpose of the 401(k) was to limit the use of executive cash deferred plans. When the 401(k) started, it was called a "salary reduction plan" which was a more honest and truthful description. After all, would American workers have ever accepted and contributed to a "salary reduction plan?" Would American workers have bought into a program the federal government called a "tax postponement" plan rather than a "tax-deferred" plan? Again, highly doubtful.

This brings us to another financial truth: "Begin with the end purpose in mind."

What is the main reason you are putting money into a 401(k), IRA, or any other tax-deferred (actually tax-postponed) retirement plan? If your answer is to build an account balance to a certain number, such as $1 million or $2 million, you may have been misled by the financial services industry.

Here's why: The true purpose of saving and investing money for retirement is to provide you and your spouse with an income stream that will continue for the rest of your lives. When it comes time to take money out of your IRA or 401(k), do you want to pay the highest amount of taxes or least amount of taxes on these distributions? Hopefully your answer is the least. Most of us have been told to contribute to these plans to "defer taxes because we'll be in a lower tax bracket in retirement."

Hopefully for you, that's not the case. Since taxes increase when income goes up, if you retire in a lower tax bracket, what does that say about your current and future lifestyle or spendable income unless you get an inheritance? It says you're broke! Or at least certainly not in a financial position to maintain your pre-retirement lifestyle for the rest of your life.

Remember, not only does the federal government dictate the tax rates you will pay at any given point, they can also change the rate at any time. What has the financial position of our government been for the past 10 to 15 years? Are they flush with cash or running annual budget deficits? Deficits. Is that Congress' fault or yours? Congress!

And hasn't the recent legislation passed to combat the financial effects of COVID-19, better known as the Coronavirus, added **trillions** of dollars to our nation's debt?

Now before you throw your hands up and wave the white flag of surrender, here are a couple of recommendations.

First, only contribute to your employer sponsored retirement plan up to the percentage of your income your employer will match.

Second, you might be saying, "But Michael, my current employer doesn't match any of my contributions. What should I do?" Contribute to your 401(k) or consider funding a traditional or Roth IRA. Your choice would depend on whether you believe income tax rates for your family will be higher or lower in the future when you withdraw money to fund your retirement. If you think tax rates will be higher, consider a Roth IRA.

Don't believe that you have to remain invested in the stock market 12 months out of the year, especially in IRA or 401(k) retirement accounts. The chart on the next page compares the average monthly performance of the S&P 500 on a price appreciation basis only (no dividends included) from 1970 to 2010.

Month	Performance Percentage	Rank
January	1.00%	4
February	-0.08%	9
March	1.11%	3
April	1.30%	2
May	0.72%	5
June	0.15%	8
July	0.44%	6
August	0.23%	7
September	-0.65%	10
October	0.44%	6
November	1.30%	2
December	1.69%	1

Source: Standard & Poor's, Inc.

As you can see, December came in first, November and April tied for second, and September came in last.

As humans, two strong emotions we possess are fear and greed. When it comes to making final financial decisions, emotions lead many of us to make mistakes. Remember the advice of Warren Buffett, one of history's most successful investors. He said (paraphrased), "Be fearful when everyone else seems to be greedy and be greedy when everyone else seems to be fearful." In chapter five, we'll also discuss my "sell strategy" I developed a few years after 2008 to help take emotion out of my selling decisions.

To reach your financial goals and dreams, I recommend a balance between growth (or risk) and guarantees (or safety). To visualize risk, picture a tank with an open top that holds all of your risky investments. That open top reminds us that our investment balances can "evaporate," or go down. We all received a dramatic reminder of this fact when the S&P 500 recently dropped from its closing price of 3,386 on February 19, 2020 and plunged over the next four and a half weeks to close at 2,237 on March 23, 2020, a 34% decrease.

To better visualize the safety component, picture a tank with a closed top that represents the fact that some savings vehicles come with guarantees. All money in our savings tank can never be lost, even due to market fluctuations. Sound appealing? Great, because we'll break down these concepts a little more in the next chapter.

CHAPTER 4

The Foundations for Building a Successful Lifetime Retirement

A funny thing happened to American workers in the 1980s. The entire retirement funding process changed significantly, and most Americans, then and now, have no idea how dramatic of a shift this change was. Let me explain.

Picture a tall snow-capped mountain. The left side of the mountain represents our working years, starting from the bottom when we get our first jobs to the top on the day we walk away from a job or a business. The right side represents our retirement years as we go down from the top of the mountain toward the bottom. The left side is the time we "accumulate" for our retirement. The right side is where we take "distributions" to provide our spendable income.

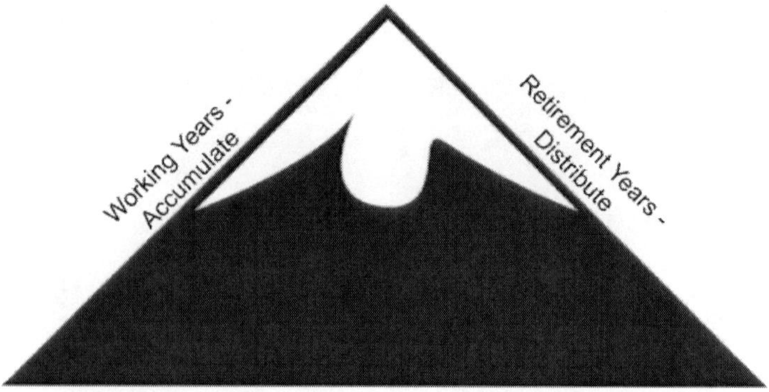

Before 1980, the majority of working Americans enjoyed a guaranteed pension, in addition to their salary, to generate retirement income for themselves. A pension simply combines one's need to accumulate money and then distributes that money to create a **guaranteed** lifetime retirement income.

And who made all the contributions? Normally, the employer. And who took all the risk of accumulating enough money to fund each worker's pension plan? The employer. Who took on all the risk of paying out the **guaranteed** amount of monthly income as long as a worker lived? Once again, the employer. To know how much to contribute each month (or year) to be able to guarantee each worker his or her lifetime retirement income, the employer used the "Law of Large Numbers."

The "Law of Large Numbers" is what's referred to as "actuarial science." According to Investopedia, actuarial science is "a discipline that applies mathematical and statistical methods to assess financial risks in the insurance and financial fields." (https://www.investopedia.com/terms/a/actuarial-science.asp).

Simply put, think of the investment industry providing the various products and strategies available for an individual or company to **accumulate** money with, and the insurance industry providing various products and strategies available for an individual or company to **distribute** money with a **guarantee**.

Then beginning in the 1980s, the 401(k) gained federal government approval and widespread acceptance, and employers quickly shifted from a guaranteed retirement income plan, or pension, to a non-guaranteed retirement savings plan, or 401(k).

Are you getting this, America? Are you beginning to realize how badly this change affects all of us? Most of us no longer have a guaranteed retirement income plan, as most working Americans are now only offered a non-guaranteed retirement savings plan.

Let me remind you that the purpose of saving and investing for retirement is not to build up the largest account balance, but to accumulate enough money to provide a lifetime retirement income for you and your spouse.

Now who makes all the contributions to your 401(k) retirement savings plan? You, the employee will make the majority, as your employer has the option, **not** the obligation, to match the dollars you contribute. Now who takes the risk of accumulating enough money to fund your retirement? You!

And how much education and training have you received concerning the products offered through your company's 401(k) plan? Enough to guarantee a lifetime retirement income for you and your spouse? And how do you calculate the amount you need to contribute each month, or each year, to allow you to fund yourself an adequate lifetime income?

Wow! How did we ever sign off on shifting all of the risks and contributions for our retirements from our employers to us individually? We didn't. The federal government, through Congress, and our employers decided for us.

So, as I see it, using a non-guaranteed 401(k) retirement savings plan instead of a pension, or guaranteed lifetime retirement income plan, comes with three additional hurdles we must all overcome.

The first hurdle is greater risk and uncertainty for you to be able to safely retire at age 65 or 70. Now you assume all of the investment and accumulation risk. You pay all the management fees that are part of all the mutual funds offered in your 401(k) plan. Using the 401(k) plan, you are willingly contributing money into a plan where you bear all the risk **and** you have no idea what the tax rate will be when you withdraw money! If that wasn't enough, the government also penalizes you if you do not withdraw your full RMD (Required Minimum

Distribution) every tax year. The penalty is 50% on the amount you did not withdraw.

The second hurdle you must overcome is one of the biggest problems with the 401(k) retirement savings plan. It is the absence of actuarial science (the "Law of Large Numbers") when an individual makes the decision of how much money can be withdrawn each year over an unknown period of time in retirement.

As individuals, we don't know what year we will die. In a pension plan, most companies would shift the distribution risk to an insurance company to fund and create an individual worker's monthly lifetime pension checks. The insurance company simply applies the "Law of Large Numbers" and their own mortality research to accurately calculate the average lifespan for the entire group of people for whom they are providing.

If you continue to use only investment industry products and strategies to provide a lifetime retirement income for yourself, you are forcing another dramatic shift in risk. Your retirement income shifts from a guaranteed-based to a probability-based plan.

Recent findings indicate an individual can only use a withdrawal rate of somewhere between 2% and 4% of their portfolio over a 20 to 30-year time period, and still have **only** about a 90% chance of not running out of money. What this means to you as an individual is this: if your retirement nest egg is $1 million, you can only withdraw between $20,000 and $40,000 per year, **and** you still have about a 10% chance of running out of money if you live 30 years into retirement.

Continuing to use an accumulation strategy while you're distributing your money to provide a monthly income was never the way retirement in the pension age worked. It's like trying to put a square peg in a round hole.

The third hurdle to overcome is known as "sequence of returns risk." If all your retirement funds are invested in stocks and bonds (accumulation products), what happens to your risk of running out of money if the market drops 10 to 20% the year you retire? The probability of running out increases the greater the percentage drop the market incurs.

Another question: Will return rates over a 15 to 30-year time period remain constant or fluctuate year by year? Returns over such a long period of time will almost certainly fluctuate, even though most charts and projections show hypothetical results based on a constant rate of return.

Let's illustrate how deceiving using a constant rate of return versus actual rate of return numbers can be. For the time period from 1970 to 1999, the average annual rate of return of the S&P 500, including dividends, was about 14.84%. Assuming a retiree had a $1 million account balance and wanted to withdraw $100,000, or 10% per year, what results did that produce using the constant rate of return of 14.84%? The table on the following page illustrates that this person would have over $15 million at the end of 30 years. Sign me up, right?

Value at beginning = $1,000,000		Annual Withdrawals = $100,000	
Length of retirement = 30 years		Average Return = 14.84%	
Constant Rate of Return Model			
Retirement Yr	**Annual Return**	**Annual Income**	**Account Value**
1	14.84%	$100,000	$1,033,560
2	14.84%	$100,000	$1,072,100
3	14.84%	$100,000	$1,116,360
4	14.84%	$100,000	$1,167,188
5	14.84%	$100,000	$1,225,558
6	14.84%	$100,000	$1,292,591
7	14.84%	$100,000	$1,369,572
8	14.84%	$100,000	$1,457,976
9	14.84%	$100,000	$1,559,500
10	14.84%	$100,000	$1,676,090
11	14.84%	$100,000	$1,809,982
12	14.84%	$100,000	$1,963,743
13	14.84%	$100,000	$2,140,322
14	14.84%	$100,000	$2,343,106
15	14.84%	$100,000	$2,575,983
16	14.84%	$100,000	$2,843,419
17	14.84%	$100,000	$3,150,542
18	14.84%	$100,000	$3,503,243
19	14.84%	$100,000	$3,908,284
20	14.84%	$100,000	$4,373,434
25	14.84%	$100,000	$7,963,668
30	14.84%	$100,000	$15,134,818

In contrast, the following chart shows the results the **same person** had using the **actual** annual returns that the S&P 500 delivered over the same 30-year time period. There's a dramatic difference. Not only is there no $15 million at the end of year 30, but this individual actually would have run out of money between year 13 and 14.

Value at beginning = $1,000,000		Annual Withdrawals = $100,000	
Length of retirement = 30 years		Average Return = 14.84%	
Actual Rate of Return Model			
Retirement Year	**Annual Return**	**Annual Income**	**Account Value**
1	3.99%	$100,000	$935,910
2	14.33%	$100,000	$955,696
3	18.94%	$100,000	$1,017,765
4	-14.79%	$100,000	$782,027
5	-26.54%	$100,000	$501,017
6	37.25%	$100,000	$550,396
7	23.67%	$100,000	$557,005
8	-7.39%	$100,000	$423,232
9	6.44%	$100,000	$344,048
10	18.35%	$100,000	$288,831
11	32.27%	$100,000	$249,767
12	5.05%	$100,000	$157,330
13	21.45%	$100,000	$69,628
14	22.50%	$100,000	-$37,206
15	6.25%	$100,000	-$145,781

As you can see, the hypothetical numbers and projections based on a constant return completely ignore the sequence of returns risk. How's that make you feel, America?

If you're ready to take back control of your retirement, email me at michael@michael-cutbirth.com and we'll get started.

CHAPTER 5

Here's What You Need to Know About Investing That You've Probably Never Been Told Before

Let's start with asking a somewhat harsh question: Is the financial investment industry interested in protecting the losses of the average investor, or is it only primarily concerned with maximizing its revenues through the fund's management fees, earned by recommending and promoting a "stay fully invested" philosophy?

Earlier I mentioned one of my financial beliefs is that we (financial advisors) can help our clients more by eliminating or reducing their losses than we ever could by trying to help them pick the winners. The following chart illustrates how much of a gain an investor would have to earn, not including fees and expenses, to compensate for various losses. Notice how the amount gained over the amount lost widens as the percentage of loss increases. In other words, the more you lose, the more you have to make just to get back to even.

If you start out even and your account drops by:	**To get back to even, you need to earn a return of:**
0%	No change
10%	11%
20%	25%
30%	45%
40%	67%
50%	100%
60%	150%
70%	233%
80%	400%
90%	900%
100%	N/A

Would you rather you, and especially your financial advisor, make financial decisions emotionally or make them logically? That's a fairly simple question, but often extremely hard to put into practice, especially during a steep market decline. Avoiding emotional responses is even more difficult the more you watch cable business shows during periods of market declines.

Want a simple "selling strategy" to help you determine when to sell an investment? First, make a list of the January 1 prices of the mutual funds or exchange-traded funds (ETFs) you own. Then, from that price, calculate a 10% decline, 15% decline, 20% decline, etc. all the way down to a 50% decline. If that position you own drops 10% during that calendar year, have an online notification service send you an email notice. If that position's price continues to fall an additional 5%, due to economic or financial reasons, sell 10% of your total position as of the previous day's value.

Once you've sold, set yourself up to "dollar cost average" back into that same mutual fund or ETF over the next six months beginning with the first day of the following month in an amount equal to what you sold out. Why average back into the same holding? Did the fund or ETF strategy stop working? I doubt it. It's much more likely something in the economy caused the stock market to cycle downward, or it just experienced a so-called "Black

Swan event" such as the global spread of the Coronavirus in 2020.

Finally, if the mutual fund or ETF continues to fall, for each additional 5% decrease after an overall 15% decline, continue to sell 10% of the previous day's total position's value. That's all there is to it.

Now, for all you visual learners, let me illustrate the last three paragraphs for you in numbers and tables.

The numbers come from my own research using the price of "ABC Growth Fund." The share price on January 1, 2008 was $33.74. Here is the price decline set up.

ABC Growth Fund (2008)				
Jan 1 Price	**-10%**	**-15%**	**-20%**	**-25%**
$33.74	$30.37	$28.68	$26.99	$25.31
-30%	**-35%**	**-40%**	**-45%**	**-50%**
$23.62	$21.93	$20.24	$18.56	$16.87

Below is my sell strategy illustrated.

Sell Strategy		
Date	**Share Price**	**Action Taken**
9/2/2008	$30.22	Down 10% - On alert
9/9/2008	$28.39	Down 15% - Sell 10%
9/29/2008	$25.94	Down 20% - Sell 10%
10/3/2008	$25.20	Down 25% - Sell 10%
10/7/2008	$22.94	Down 30% - Sell 10%
10/9/2008	$21.60	Down 35% - Sell 10%
10/24/2008	$20.16	Down 40% - Sell 10%
11/20/2008	$17.41	Down 45% - Sell 10%

Assuming we had $10,000 worth of ABC Growth Fund on September 8, 2008, the total sales in September 2008 would have been approximately $830 on September 9 and $750 on September 29 for a total of $1,580. Dividing $1,580 by six equals $263.33. This means you would have bought $263 worth of ABC Growth Fund on September 1, October 1, and December 1 of 2008, and January 1, February 1, and March 1 of 2009. This calculation was repeated for October and November 2008 as illustrated on the next page.

Fund Sales					
September	**Amount**	**October**	**Amount**	**November**	**Amount**
9/8/2008	$830	10/3/2008	$625	11/20/2008	$340
9/29/2008	$750	10/7/2008	$530		$340
	$1,580	10/9/2008	$450	$340 / 6 =	$56.67
$1,580 / 6 =	$263.33	10/24/2008	$370		
			$1,975		
		$1,975 / 6 =	$329.17		

The total monthly repurchases of ABC Growth Fund from October 2008 to May 2009 are illustrated below:

Fund Repurchases				
10/1/2008	**11/1/2008**	**12/1/2008-3/1/2009**	**4/1/2009**	**5/1/2009**
$263.33	$263.33	263.33	$329.17	$56.67
	$329.17	$329.17	$56.67	
	$592.50	$56.67	$385.84	
		$649.17		

**Past performance does not guarantee future results.*

If you followed my sell strategy in 2008, your ABC Growth Fund holding would have returned to $10,000 of value in February 2011. If you had applied a "buy and hold" strategy your ABC Growth Fund holding would have returned to $10,000 13 months later in March 2012. In addition, your stress level would have been less during the period of market declines because you took action.

Here's another rule to follow: Never fall in love with a single stock. If you don't believe me, ask the former employees of Enron, who had a large percentage of their retirement plan holdings in company stock when the proverbial "you-know-what" hit the fan. It was tragic and criminal, but they had no recourse when the company went bankrupt.

A more recent example involves the current and former employees of Exxon Mobil. Think how nervous they must be if they relied on Exxon company stock to fund the majority of their retirement plans. From January 2010 to March of 2020, the only time the stock price fell below $60 was in June of 2010, before it closed at $59.88 on February 18, 2020. The stock continued to tumble to a low of $30.11 on March 23, 2020. Never fall in love with a single stock.

Here's a question with an easy answer: how do you maximize your gains while investing in the stock market? Buy low and sell high. Sounds simple, but consider this: if an investor reinvested all dividends and capital gains generated by his or her mutual fund holdings since March 2009, did they buy low? No, they didn't. They started out buying low but after a while, they bought higher and higher and higher as the market went up and up.

This leads to a more difficult question of "When should I sell?" The answer depends partially on how greedy you are. It also depends on if you've taken the emotion out of how much you'll let a particular holding of yours increase before you start to take some profits.

I fell victim to this myself. A particular client I inherited had about 80% of his retirement fund in a single mutual fund. Normally not a smart strategy, but here's how the story unfolded: Since 2009, the fund only had two down years, 2011 when it lost almost 7%, and 2018, when it was down a little less than 4%. Both of these were minor losses. Leading up to this, the fund had averaged an annual return of about 10.7% for the past 10 years, so I advised this client to keep riding the fund up until the cycle headed downward. I never expected a virus to cause the stock market to drop over 30% in five weeks. Nobody would, right? Ease my guilt...please!

Here's a bit more of the story: The fund's 2017 return was about 27%. It was negative 3.8% in 2018, up over 36% in 2019, and was up **another** 7.5% after the first three weeks of 2020. I kicked myself several times a day for not taking some of those profits off the table. For goodness sake, the fund was up 67% from January 2017 to January 2020. How much further could it go up considering February has historically been the second worst performing month of the year?

I encourage you to think logically as you take a lesson from this story. If you were gambling on a roulette wheel and bet $100,000 on a single roll and won $27,000 (think 27% gain from the above fund in 2017), would you let it ride or would you take some of the profits off the table? If you won an additional $33,000, would you have left $160,000 at risk? No one in their right mind would, but this client of mine did. That's the lesson I learned from the 2020 market decline. The good news is that his fund is only down about 7.5% year-to-date, as of April 15, 2020.

Here's another question: Does market timing work? The answer depends on who you ask. My answer would be, "Absolutely, yes." The vast majority of financial advisors would answer with an emphatic "No." (Probably a, "Heck, no.") Their proof would probably be one of those infamous charts that demonstrates how much less an investor would have earned had they missed the best 10, 20, and 40 days in the market over the last 20 or so years.

The registered investment advisory (RIA) firm I work with uses a seasonal timing strategy, similar to one that limited investors' losses to less than 4% in 2008 during the financial crisis. This compares to a loss of over 30% for the Dow Jones Industrial Average, a loss of over 36% for the S&P 500, and a loss of a little over 40% for the NASDAQ. For the 10-year return period beginning in 1999, the timing strategy's return was more than twice the Dow Jones Industrial Average.

If this timing strategy sounds attractive to you, it's probably time we connect. Email me at michael@michael-cutbirth.com.

CHAPTER 6

The Five Major Areas of Wealth Transfer

I'm often asked the question, "What do you do?" I smile, and oftentimes say something like, "I've never had more fun in my life than I'm having right now. But before I answer your question, let me tell you what I believe."

I go on to say, "I believe every person in this country only needs to pay taxes on their money one time. Just once. That's as they earn it. And I believe people ought to be in control of their hard-earned money, not the federal government, Wall Street, or the financial institutions you and I deal with every day." Following a little chuckle, I continue, "I mean, do you really think they have your best interests at heart? Do you really think they designed the rules so you and I win?"

"I teach people how they can recover tens of thousands of dollars a year they don't even know they're losing because they're simply chasing rates of return. In fact, just last year, the people we worked with had about twenty to as much as $50,000 or more slipping right through their fingers because they didn't understand how damaging interest, taxes, and fees were to their financial situations."

So my question to them, and to you, is this, "If I sat down with you and we found anywhere near $30,000 of your money that you were losing, would you want it back?"

Now, let's briefly review the five major areas of wealth transfers. A wealth transfer occurs when people use money or pay for a large purchase in such a way that, when added together, they're losing tens of thousands of dollars unknowingly and unnecessarily. Unknowingly means you're forgiven; you don't even know you're doing it. Unnecessarily means we can stop it and fix it.

The first area of wealth transfer is how you pay for your house. Many people believe that paying off their houses quickly saves them interest. As a result, they choose a 15-year loan, or pay $200 to $500 a month extra on the mortgage if they have a 30-year loan. In their defense, the bank or mortgage company has probably shown them how much interest could be saved by doing so. Just like the financial services industry only shows what an investor loses by missing the best days in the market, interest savings on a loan or mortgage is only half of the story.

Because of that, I have a couple of questions for you: First, if mortgage interest is an available tax deduction for your family, how much of a deduction do you want? The least amount or the greatest amount? Second, how long do you want to take advantage of that tax deduction? For a few years or over an extended period of time?

Don't misunderstand. I want you, and every client, to have a paid-off house as quickly as possible. The difference is that I teach clients strategies to help them take advantage of the mortgage interest deduction, while maintaining liquidity, use, and control of their money, or the "LUC factor." Since you're still reading this, I'm betting you are a person who likes to be in control of your money instead of out of control with your money.

The second area of wealth transfer is how much you pay in income taxes. As previously discussed, paying off your mortgage early eliminates your mortgage interest deduction which can increase the amount of taxes you pay. Another way many people pay more than necessary in taxes is by reinvesting dividends and capital gains on non-retirement investment account holdings. Oftentimes, after 15 to 20 years, the amount one owes in extra taxes is $1,000 or more.

The third area of wealth transfer is how you fund your qualified plan or retirement accounts. Simply put, contributing to your employer sponsored retirement plans (i.e. 401(k), SIMPLE IRA, etc.) over the company match will also likely increase the amount of taxes you pay in the future.

Often when I meet with a client, and we're finding money slipping through their fingers, they tell me they owe $10,000 to $20,000 on credit cards. When I ask what interest rate they're paying, 99 times out of 100 they can't tell me. Upon researching, the interest charges often average between 10% to 15% or more. Does not knowing make the interest expense go down? Definitely not.

When I ask these same people how much they're contributing to their 401(k)s, they answer, "$18,000," or that year's max contribution. I nicely educate them about the effect these two wealth transfers have. On one hand, they're trying to decrease taxes by putting more money in their 401(k)s. On the other hand, the amount of monthly interest they're paying to the credit card company probably exceeds the gain earned - over and above the company match - on their 401(k) contributions. Quick solution? Stop overfunding your 401(k) and pay off your credit cards.

Would you ever think of driving down the freeway with your right foot pressing the accelerator while, at the same time, you're pressing the brake with your left foot? Ridiculous, right? You would be stuck, not going anywhere, and you'd be putting yourself in danger. What's the difference between driving like that and funding your 401(k) while carrying tens of thousands of dollars in credit card debt? Not much.

The fourth area of wealth transfer is how you pay for a major capital purchase. I define a major capital purchase as anything you cannot afford to pay, in full, from your monthly cash flow. Two primary examples are buying a new car and paying the wedding expenses for your child. Too many people simply use a credit card or go to the bank and borrow the money, and then make monthly payments until the debt is finally paid off years later. This results in hundreds, if not thousands, of dollars in wealth transfer costs.

The fifth area of wealth transfer is paying for your children's college expenses. This is definitely an area where many people transfer tens of thousands of dollars, even if they use a 529 plan that funds the entire cost.

Most parents leave no stone unturned when they stress over how to pay for their children's college education. Many borrow from their 401(k) plans or take IRA withdrawals, costing income taxes, all while putting their retirement goals in danger. Or, in their desperation for solutions, they load up on Parent PLUS loans to the point where these loan payments equal or exceed their monthly mortgage payments.

Now, you may wonder how in the world could a wealth transfer take place if a parent is fortunate enough to be able to pay for their child's college education with money withdrawn from a 529 College

Savings Plan? The simple answer is you can't put the money back in the 529 Plan to continue to compound and grow to supplement your retirement like you could if you took a margin loan against a non-529 Plan investment account.

Would you like some help planning for how to pay for your children's college education expenses? My good friend and colleague, Beth Walker, and I would love to take this stress and worry off of you! Visit www.CenterForCollegeSolutions.com. Under the "Services" tab you'll find a brief summary of the proven steps we use to get your child in the "right" school for the "right" price. These steps are fully explained in her book, "Never Pay Retail for College," available by clicking on the "Book" tab. Be sure and tell her Michael Cutbirth from Texas recommended you.

CHAPTER 7

Helpful Hints You May Have Never Heard----Points to Ponder

Many people become confused when it comes to paying their mortgages. Let me ask you this: when you buy a house, are you ever really in debt? Unless we have another downturn in the real estate market like 2008, shouldn't the value of your house plus your down payment be equal to or exceed the mortgage balance on your house at any point in time? If so, how can a mortgage ever be a real debt? I don't consider a mortgage to be a debt, but rather an obligation you have to a mortgage company for an asset you've purchased.

How much interest does your house make? Zero. The equity in your house appreciates at a 0% rate of return. Don't believe me? Consider this. You and I are neighbors and own identical homes. Let's say both of our houses are valued at $350,000. Let's further assume you paid $300,000 cash for your house, and I still owe $250,000 on the mortgage. Did your house grow in value any differently than mine? Did your house not appreciate in value from $300,000 to $350,000, just like mine? The house's value is just based on location, location, location.

Let's dig a little deeper into this scenario. Assume I have an investment or savings account valued at $250,000. Don't I, in essence, have a paid-off house? I would suggest the answer is, "Absolutely." Why? Because, if I choose, I could write a check at any time and pay off my mortgage.

Why might I choose to have a mortgage rather than a paid-off house? Because of the tradeoff I'd be making. How much should I be able to earn with my $250,000 worth of investments over the next 30 years? Assuming a moderate 6% rate of return, my $250,000 (not including taxes or any other expenses), would grow to a little over $1.4 million. Do you think your $350,000 house would be worth $1.4 million in 30 years? Do you realize the tremendous amount of future wealth you voluntarily missed out on or "transferred away" by paying cash for your house?

Let's shift gears. One of the worst pieces of financial advice I ever received came from a manager I worked with. He recommended I trade-in my car every three years, buying a nicer car each time to impress my potential clients. Would you believe I didn't even know what a car title looked like until I was almost 45? That's when I paid off my first car loan, and it pains me to think of all of that money I wasted, even today.

Let's calculate what that would cost a person who applied that philosophy. Let's assume we buy a $25,000 car and finance it for five years but trade it in every three years for another $25,000 car over a 30-year time period. Let's also assume a 5% interest rate on the car payment, and the same 5% interest if we were able to invest all the loan interest over those 30 years. What would the wealth transfer total at a 5% rate of return? $74,000. If we were able to earn a 7% rate of return over those 30 years, the wealth transfer would total over $110,000. That's a lot of money transferred out of your pocket. Plus, nicer cars also come with higher car insurance, repair parts, and repair costs as well.

Here's a final point to ponder: What does it mean to you when a financial advisor or TV spokesperson tells you that the average return on "ABC mutual fund" was 10.5% over the past 10 years? You probably think, "Why didn't I invest in ABC mutual fund 10 years ago?" Afterall, if you apply the "Rule of 72," your money doubles every seven years at 10%. You're thinking, "The money I could have invested would have more than doubled!"

What that really means is if you invested a single sum 10 years ago, without adding to or subtracting from your investment, not taking into account sales charges, taxes, or fund expenses, your account would have averaged 10.5% over that period. Is that how we invest money, America? Absolutely not. We add to our 401(k) holdings monthly, and the mutual fund industry has programmed us to "dollar cost average" into our "non-qualified," or cash, accounts, too. The 10-year average rate of return of 10.5% is the truth, but not the entire truth. It's certainly not based on how most of us actually invest our money.

CONCLUSION

In summary, let me give you an example that will quickly show how deceptive illustrated rates of return can be for the unenlightened. Let's say I come to you with the following: "Dear reader, I have an incredible investment opportunity for you. It's a two-year investment and I guarantee - yes **guarantee** - you a 20% average rate of return."

I have two questions for you: (1) Would you like to invest? (2) Is it possible you could lose money? I suspect you would probably answer, "Yes" to the first question and, after thinking about the second question a little bit (since I just explained that average annual rate of return doesn't mean much), you'd probably answer, "I hope not" or "I wouldn't think so."

See the table on the next page.

Year	Beginning Balance	Return	Gain/Loss	Ending Balance
Year 1	$100	100%	$100	$200
Year 2	$200	-60%	-$120	$80

Adding the two years' returns of 100% and negative 60% mathematically equals 40%. When you divide 40% by two (for the number of years), it equals 20%. As you can see, you could have a "20% average rate of return" and still lose money. Don't think a mutual fund can make that much in a year and lose that much the following year? Dear reader, it can happen and has happened before. I know of a technology fund that gained a little over 100% in 1999 and lost almost that exact same 100% the following year, 2000, during the tech bubble.

Has your current financial advisor asked you the four toughest financial questions we all face?

1. Do you know what rate of return you have to earn on your assets to be able to retire at your current standard of living and have your money last through your life expectancy?

2. Do you know how much you need to save on a monthly or annual basis to be able to retire at your current standard of living and have your money last as long as you do?

3. Doing what you are currently doing, how long will you have to work to be able to retire and live your current lifestyle through your life expectancy?

4. If you don't do anything differently than what you're doing today, how much will you have to reduce your current standard of living at retirement for your money to last to your life expectancy?

I can give you these answers in about 10 to 15 minutes. When do you want to know?

As I reach the end of this book, I wish to sincerely thank you for sticking it out to the end. This journey, the continuous searching for and seeking of truth, has fueled my desire to be a lifelong learner. This journey has taught me to listen, truly listen, to my clients. Their financial goals are not mine, as my financial goals are not theirs. This journey continues to remind me to ensure I follow my own advice: take profits off the table, plan how to minimize losses, and never fall in love with a particular stock, mutual fund, or ETF.

My sincere hope for each of you is that **some** portion of this book's message struck a nerve and had you thinking, "He's right. That makes so much sense. Why hasn't anyone told me that before? I need to stop doing that."

Always remember these three irrefutable truths:

1. The house always wins
2. He who has the gold (i.e. the federal government) makes the rules
3. Investing in the stock market is just a form of legalized gambling

Finally, begin with the end purpose in mind. When it comes to retirement savings, the winners are the people who turn their account balances into a guaranteed lifetime monthly income for themselves and their spouses. It's not necessarily the person who has the largest account balance.

If you'd like to start a conversation to discuss any questions or concerns you may have about achieving your financial goals and dreams, send me a message at michael@michael-cutbirth.com.

"You shall know the truth, and the truth shall set you free."

ABOUT THE AUTHOR

Michael P. Cutbirth has been in the financial services industry for 35 years. After 2008, he realized the entire investment world had changed, but the recommendations coming from financial institutions, Wall Street, and the government stayed the same. When he's not actively pursuing his mission to bring financial truths to his clients, he spends time with his wife, Dana, in Richmond, TX, and loves spoiling his grandchildren.

Made in United States
North Haven, CT
04 November 2026

21768940R00049